summercrafts

summercrafts

Fun and Creative Projects for the Whole Family

marjorie galen

HYLAS

Irvington, NY

HYLAS

Hylas Publishing
129 Main Street
Irvington, New York 10533
www.hylaspublishing.com

Hylas Publishing
Publisher: Sean Moore
Creative Director: Karen Prince
Art Directors: Edwin Kuo, Gus Yoo
Editorial Director: Lori Baird

Project Credits
Editor: Gail Greiner
Assistant Editor: Angda Goel
Designer: Shamona Stokes
Production Manager: Sarah Reilly
Illustrator: Jason Lee

ISBN: 1-59258-131-5

Library of Congress Cataloging-in-Publication Data available upon request.

Photography © Marjorie Galen
Additional photography (pages 26–28, 45–46, 49, 53) © Karen Prince
Author photo by Gail Greiner

Printed and bound in Italy
Distributed by National Book Network

First American Edition published in 2005

10 9 8 7 6 5 4 3 2 1

To my kids,
Ike and Ellie Kitman,
and
to the memory
of my grandmother
Lillian Brager

contents...

introduction...

This book of projects is inspired by all the days I've spent at the beach, all the hours I've walked along the Hudson River by my house, and all the time I've spent making things with my children and our friends. This is not a book just for kids, nor is it a book just for grownups. I like to think of it as a book for the whole family. Smaller children will need more help, but everyone can get involved with nearly every project. Although some of the projects may require a trip to your favorite (or closest) waterfront spot, most of the crafts can be done just about anywhere.

When I was a little girl, my grandparents lived near the beach, but my first beach memories are not what you'd think: they are not summer memories. The beach in winter is what I remember most clearly. Back then—do they still do this now?—whoever took care of the beach tucked it into a turbulent winter bed by piling the sand high so the stormy ocean couldn't drag the beach out to sea. Those dunes were probably not very big, but I was little and to me they were mountains—mountains I could climb to the very top and slide down safely, laughing the whole way, sand pouring in the tops of my red rubber boots until they were full.

I love water, and I am so happy to live just up the hill from the Hudson, the wide river that flows from Lake Tear of the Clouds, past New York City, and into the Atlantic Ocean. Winter or summer, my favorite kind of vacation still involves going to the beach.

That said, I'm not a surfer or a kayaker, I know that I shouldn't get too much of a tan, and I hate to sit still. At the beach, or along the riverbank, when I'm not making sure my children don't get swept out to sea or kidnapped by tugboat pirates, I spend my time collecting: shells, rocks, feathers, bits of broken pottery, and smooth sea glass. And I make things. I sew or knit or build sculptures, and I dig holes in the sand with my kids.

My grandmother loved the beach, too. She loved the sound and the smell and the look of the water. When I was young, she would hold her largest conch shell to my ear and ask me what I heard: a whishing sound so much like the ocean that I would peer inside again and again trying to see what made the noise.

My grandmother was a sculptor on the side—on the side of being cook, homemaker, cheese sandwich maker, and general constant cheerful presence. My first craft project—with her in her basement workroom—was marbleized paper. We floated droplets of oil paint on a tray of water, dropped a piece of paper on top, and lifted it up to find that, magically, the color had stuck: beautiful swirls of color, crazy patterns that I could attach to the page; better even than crayons. I was hooked.

For the rest of her life, my grandmother continued to be interested in my craft projects, and she saved every single card and drawing I ever made for her. It was nice to have a fan. Our final project together, before she died, was a knitted blanket. She had moved

away from her house on the bay and near the beach, and down to Florida with my grandfather years before. I sent her knitting needles, wool in all different colors, and the request that she knit squares the same size as mine. We knitted away in different states with a single goal: a large blanket to wrap around my children at story time. We were knitting pen pals.

When I think about the book you are holding in your hands, my biggest hope is that it will not only provide you and your children with the skills and the inspiration to make whatever you can imagine, but that the process of creating will bring you and your kids together and start you all on a lifelong journey of making things. My other big hope is that you will feel free to improvise. This, to me, is more important than following the directions letter by letter for any particular project. Kids have creative minds and great ideas, and with a little help they can create wonderful objects. I hope you and your family will be inspired by your summer holiday, whether it's a month at the seaside, a day at a lake, an afternoon on a riverbank, or just some time off from school in your own backyard. Spend some time together making mermaids or sea monkeys, writing vacation storybooks or collecting shells for your memory box, sewing backpacks or sail or totes, building boats or blocks or backgammon boards…whatever catches your eye and fires your imagination.

how to use this book

Use this book as a guide, a place to get started thinking about what you and your kids want to make. The surest way to kill children's creativity is to tell them they are doing something the wrong way. And the surest way to avoid trying altogether (this is for the adults among you) is to think that your finished project has to be perfect. I am very happy with the projects in this book, but I can tell you honestly that I went down many wrong roads and "wasted" a lot of time on projects that just didn't work out—and I had a great time doing it. Immersing yourself in a creative puzzle is meditative and restorative.

Feel free to substitute materials used here for whatever you can find easily. Explore your local art and craft stores, knitting and needlework stores, and hardware store. Something will inspire you. And, if you look, you will probably find cool things around the house that can be given a new life.

Hot Rocks

At first I made hot rocks all wrong. My friend Elizabeth had described her favorite beach project to me over the phone. She said, "Color on the rocks with crayons, then put them in the oven." Or at least that's what I thought she said. I did that, and the results were okay, nothing special. The rocks that came out of the oven looked about the same as the rocks that had gone in. Luckily, I went to visit Elizabeth at the beach for a lesson in making hot rocks. There, in a fabulous shingled beach house that looked like it should be in a movie, I got a demonstration from the experts. Elizabeth, her daughter, and her nieces taught me the secret to making perfect hot rocks: you heat the rocks first! It makes all the difference. The crayons melt on the rocks as you draw, leaving thick lines of luminous wax behind. It's like painting with luscious oil paints, but without any of the control problems—the colors don't get muddy. And the smell is fantastic, like being in a crayon factory. The little bit of hot air that rises from the rocks makes this a good project for a cool summer day, of which there are plenty at the beach. As far as I know, Elizabeth's family invented hot rocks, and I am impressed. The process is magical and the outcome is beautiful; I predict that the adults will still be making hot rocks long after the kids have left for the beach. Just tell them not to go into the water until you are finished. They may have to wait awhile!

what you need

- Oven and oven mitts
- Smooth stones…large flat stones work best because they hold the heat but are not too heavy when piled onto the cookie sheet
- Cookie sheet…covered with wax paper, foil, or parchment if you are picky about your cookie sheets
- Crayons

how to...

...make hot rocks

1 Preheat the oven to 350°F.

2 Arrange one layer of stones on your cookie sheet and place it in the oven.

3 While the stones are heating, peel the paper off your crayons (a good job for the youngest among you).

4 When the rocks are hot, after about 15 minutes, remove them from the oven and, with an oven mitt, spread them out on a heat-proof surface. We took ours outside onto the flagstone patio. A picnic table would work, too.

WARNING: The stones are hot. Don't touch them with your bare hands. Use an oven mitt.

5 Start to color on the stones right away, but be careful as they will hold their heat for longer than you think. Keep coloring for as long as you like (and as long as the wax still melts); the more color the better.

Seashells & Rocks

My favorite thing to do with seashells, rocks, and sea glass is to collect them, put them in a bowl or on a tray, and admire them. I regularly walk down to the Hudson River with my kids, and inevitably we come back with a few more pieces of broken pottery or sea glass. I rarely come home from a trip to the beach without bags full of shells and rocks. Exploring nature, collecting its treasures, and using them to decorate your home is what this section is all about. And I confess, much as I love seashell collages, I really love Mod-Podge® (a great decoupage product that I always—mistakenly I now see—called "modge podge"). I Mod-Podged a bit as a kid but hadn't given it a thought until a few years back when a friend went on a binge. She Mod-Podged her telephone, her medicine chest, every switch plate in her apartment, and finally the globelike vases for her wedding. I helped with the wedding vases—we covered them with old road maps—and was hooked. As you can see from the examples here, anything goes…pick a photo of a friend, a rock star, or your favorite politician, or just make a design with pretty paper. I Mod-Podged small rocks to use as playing pieces for my chess- and checkerboard project. I keep dreaming about Mod-Podging my kitchen cabinets, but I'm hoping to talk myself out of it.

what you need

You will need some or all of these things, depending on what you are making:

- Paper…anything thin will do: newspaper, magazine pages, origami paper, tissue paper
- Paintbrush
- Mod-Podge (or white craft glue; see note)
- Seashells
- Rocks
- Paint…poster paint works well; so does acrylic paint
- Fine-point permanent marker
- Aleene's® Original "Tacky" Glue™ (I find this works best for making collages and gluing shells to picture frames); you can also use a hot glue gun if you have one
- Picture frame
- Driftwood or an old board

NOTE: If you can't find Mod-Podge, you can dilute white craft glue with water (three parts glue to one part water).

how to...

...use Mod-Podge

1 Cut up your paper. You can cut a photo into pieces or just cut your paper into shapes. Mod-Podge works best with smallish pieces, and even a larger photo will still read if it's cut up and pieced back together. Plus it will look cool.

2 With your paint brush, brush a little Mod-Podge onto your shell or rock.

3 Start placing your paper, a few pieces at a time, and brush more Mod-Podge over the top. Make sure the paper is smooth and all the edges are glued down.

4 Keep layering and Mod-Podging until you are finished.

...make things with shells & rocks

ROCK PLACE CARDS. Turn rocks into place cards for a tea party or a fancy dinner. Paint the name of each guest on a large smooth stone. I painted my rocks with silver acrylic paint first, and waited for the paint to dry before I painted the names. Don't make the mistake I did and use oil paint for the names; it takes days to dry, and you'll have to postpone your party. Decorate the rocks with flowers, curlicues, whatever you like. At the end of the party, your friends can take the rocks home as favors.

SALT HOLDER. A clamshell makes a perfect salt holder. Salt and a loaf of bread is a traditional Russian housewarming gift, to ensure that the newcomers will never be without the necessities of life. (Did you know that salt was once such a valuable commodity that the word *salary* derives from the Latin word for *salt*?) Wash a large white clamshell and fill it with sea salt. Kids love to help themselves to salt from the shell. If you like, you can add a much smaller clamshell to use as a scoop, but most people just use their fingers. Give one as a gift, or just use it at home.

how to...

SEA GLASS COLLECTION. Start a sea glass collection...Pick a bowl and add your sea glass findings every time you go to the beach or the river's edge. Throw back any pieces with sharp edges—they aren't fully "cooked"; they need to be smoothed by the sand and the water. Keep adding to your collection.

FAMILY TREE. Make a family tree. Using a permanent marker, draw cartoony pictures of your family members, pets, and friends on small, smooth rocks. Glue them to a board using "Tacky" Glue or a hot glue gun.

PICTURE FRAME. Collect lots of small shells, and glue them onto a picture frame using "Tacky" Glue or a hot glue gun. Let dry. Frame a photo of your family at the beach. Grandparents love these, but make a few, because you won't want to give them all away.

COLLAGE. Make a collage…to celebrate a birthday, commemorate your sailboat, write your name in broken pieces of seashells, or just express yourself. A piece of driftwood or an old board works well as a background. Use "Tacky" Glue or a hot glue gun to attach the shells.

CHESS/CHECKER SET. Decorate enough small rocks for chess (32) or checkers (24) or backgammon (30) in two colors. Mod-Podge works well; so does paint, or you can make hot rocks. For chess, you can draw kings, queens, and so forth, or just create your own designs.

Mobiles

I remember the disappointment I felt when I was small if I didn't find perfect shells as I walked along the beach with my bucket. The ones that were broken or had holes in them were considered substandard and were rejected. For mobiles, shells with holes are coveted—in fact, they're necessary if you want to hang the shells on a piece of string. You will find out who your friends really are when you ask to use a particularly beautiful piece of holey shell from someone else's pile. My friend Gail has a big collection of shells stashed in a corner of her beach house deck. She gave me a superb dark grey oyster shell (with a hole in it) for a mobile I was making. You can't count on everyone to be so generous, however, so you will have to do most of your shell gathering yourself. It's part of the fun anyway.

Take a beach bag, maybe even one you've made (see the grommet backpack and sailor tote projects), and head to the beach to collect things. Look for particularly nice pieces of driftwood and, of course, shells with holes in them so you can string them up and hang them on your mobile— or give them to a friend in need. Some beaches are low on driftwood, so a dead pine bough may have to suffice.

A group of us have been making mobiles together for a few summers now, always using just plain fishing line to hang the shells. This past summer, one of us combined mobile making with one of our other beach-time passions—beading—and created a masterpiece, covering the fishing line with colorful glass beads. It started a revolution, and our windows haven't been the same since.

what you need

- Driftwood or any piece of wood you like
- Fishing line
- Seashells with holes in them
- Small screw eyes (optional)
- Beads (optional; see page 112 for techniques)
- Poster paint (optional)

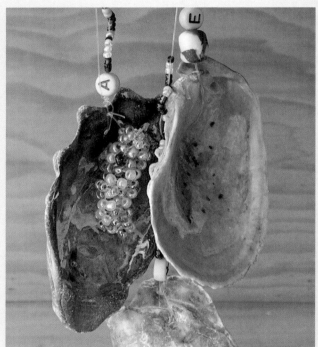

how to...

...make a mobile

Balance is important when making a mobile. Think of the great mobile maker Alexander Calder. His mobiles are made of large, heavy pieces of metal, yet they hang perfectly in balance. Keep this in mind when making your mobile and lift it up to check its balance every once in awhile. You'll find that it's the need for balance that inspires the design.

1 Start with a piece of wood. Tie some fishing line to the center of the wood, so the mobile can hang and you can check the balance from the very beginning. Or you can screw a small screw eye into the top of the wood and tie the fishing line to that.

2 Tie a shell or shells onto a length of fishing line. The key to securing fishing line is a triple knot.

3 Tie the string onto your piece of wood.

4 Continue adding strings with shells until your mobile is done.

5 For extra pizzazz, add beads to your mobile strings. You can try the wavy beading technique (see page 113) or add letter beads to spell out a name or a message.

1

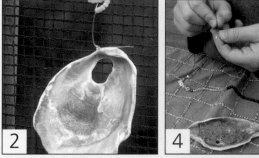

2

4

5

have a scavenger hunt...

Make a list of things to find at the beach, give copies to your friends, and head out to search for sea glass, feathers, certain kinds of shells, discarded beach fencing, driftwood, and so on. Whoever finds it all first wins, but everyone is guaranteed to have a great time.

No starfish were harmed in the making of this book!

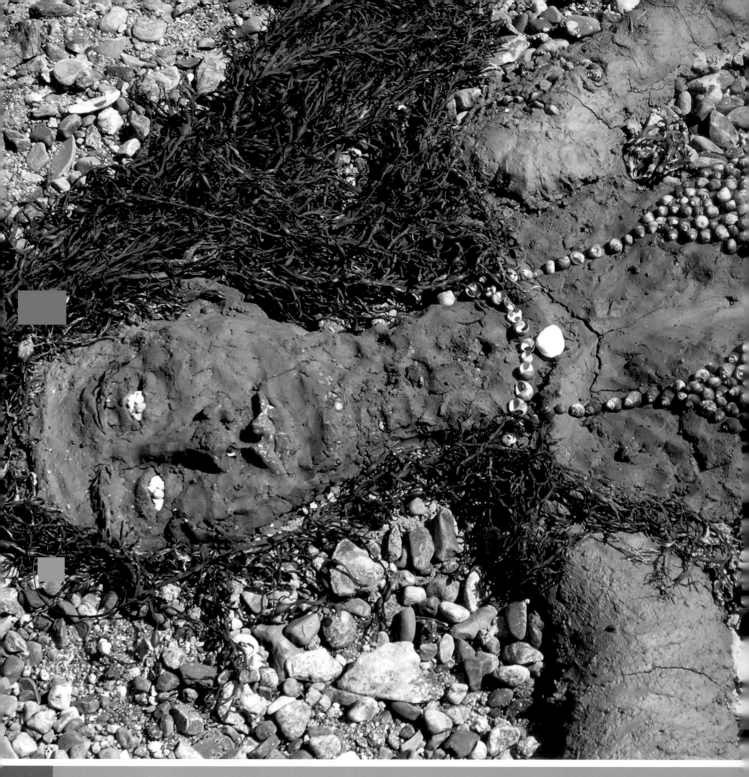

4

Beach Sculptures

When I go to the beach I don't think about surfing or even swimming. I think about what kinds of materials are there and what I can make with them. One morning, my friend Suzanna, her son Walker, and I decided to make a mermaid on their clay beach, on the banks of a wide tidal river. A mussel bed is just off the shore, so thousands of mussel shells wash up on their beach, as well as lots of little striped periwinkle shells. The mussel shells made us think of a shimmery mermaid's tail, and the periwinkle shells were perfect for the bikini top. We sculpted her body out of clay, which baked half the day in the sun, making our mermaid look ancient and wise.

On a very different kind of beach—sand and rocks, and more rocks— some friends and I made a big peace sign out of large rocks and a big plank we found washed up on shore. We were hoping to send a message to any passing planes.

Your beach sculpture doesn't need to be elaborate. Sand castles—with or without fancy moats—are a tried and true expression of time well spent at the beach. One morning, my son Ike and I decided to go geometric and made a spiral using only the smallest white shells, starting in the center and going round and round until we were out of shells and energy, and ready for lunch.

There is something very satisfying about making something on the beach, even though you know it's not forever, or maybe because you know it's not forever. Your sculpture will wash away, and become part of nature again. When our mermaid washed away, there were tears in our eyes, but they were happy tears.

what you need

- Rocks
- Seashells
- Seaweed
- Driftwood
- Feathers

...some or all of these things, whatever you can find…anything natural. Remember that your sculpture will most likely wash back into the ocean, so it's important not to add anything that will pollute the water.

how to...

...make beach sculptures

1 Look at your ocean, river, or lake beach. What do you see? Are there lots of large rocks or an abundance of mussel shells? Do you see seashells and seaweed, or just sand, sand, and more sand?

2 Think of something you want to make, and get started. If you can't think of anything, try a mermaid, a giant squid, a seahorse, or a sand sculpture of your dog. Anything goes. Remember to check the tide charts so you'll know how long you have to work before your masterpiece gets washed away.

3 Photograph your beach sculpture before it washes away.

Grommet Backpacks

Suzanna and I were sitting on the rock-strewn clay beach in front of her summer cottage, drinking coffee and talking about the backpacks we wanted to make that day. Our kids were up in Walker's tree house tossing pine cones and suggestions (some helpful, some not so much) our way. I planned to use grommets because grommets remind me of sailboats (grommets are used on sails to reinforce the places where the sails are tied to the mast) and so does this stretch of fir tree-studded coast. Suzanna came up with the idea of combining the grommet with a little turned-up corner…also very nautical (for more nautical corners, see the sailor tote). Use your backpack to take your book and sun block to the beach, for collecting shells and driftwood, or—as Walker does—for carrying around your candy. I made one from corduroy, so I can use it all year long.

The small size is perfect for children, teenage girls, and adults who want a small bag. The large size is good for anyone who has a bit more to carry. Most any fabric works, so your backpack can be classic or outrageous. Look around the house and you may find some interesting fabric begging to be turned into a backpack.

My favorite backpacks and sailor totes are the ones made from towels my dad (who was in the radio business) got from rock radio stations in the sixties and seventies. They are emblazoned with guitars, girls in bikinis, swirly flowers, and the names of rock bands such as The Who and Santana. I used the towels for years as a child at the local pool, and now they make great bags.

what you need

Two sizes…Small measures 10½" wide x 15" tall finished. Large measures 15" wide x 18" tall finished.

- One piece of fabric measuring 11½" x 34" for the small backpack (16" x 42" for the large)…most anything works: canvas, cotton, an old towel or sheet, corduroy

- Chalk (or a pencil) to mark seams and grommet placement

- Needle (if you are using stiff material, use a heavy-duty needle)

- Thread

- Pins

- ⅜" Grommets (11 total) and a grommet setter (see note)

- Hammer or mallet

- Straps…Twill binding tape from the fabric store works well; so does rope or sailing line. My favorite straps were made from colorful mountain-climbing rope I bought at a sporting goods store. Strap size depends on the size of the person wearing the backpack; for a large child you will need about 70".

NOTE: You can find grommets at most hardware and sewing stores, but if you can't or don't want to, you can hand sew round buttonholes. *See below:*

how to...

...make a grommet backpack

Instructions for the small backpack are included, with any differences for the large backpack noted in parentheses.

1 Fold the fabric, right sides together, at the center.

2 Make a chalk line ½" from the edge along the sides of the backpack. Sew along this line using a back stitch. Keep your stitches small so that the seam will be strong and the things in your backpack won't pop out the sides. If you want your seam to be extra-strong, you can stitch two lines right next to each other.

3 Cut a small triangle at the bottom corners near the fold so when you turn the backpack right side out, the corners will be as crisp and square as possible. Be careful not to cut into the line of stitching.

diagrams

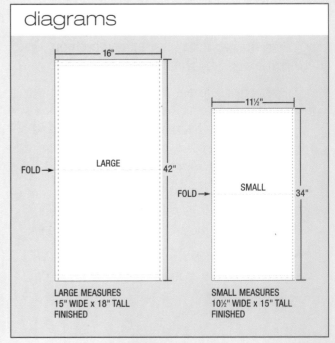

16"

FOLD → LARGE 42"

LARGE MEASURES
15" WIDE x 18" TALL
FINISHED

11½"

FOLD → SMALL 34"

SMALL MEASURES
10½" WIDE x 15" TALL
FINISHED

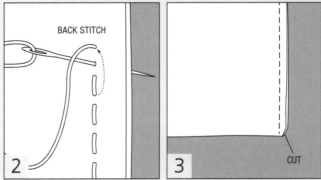

BACK STITCH

2

3

CUT

4 With the backpack still inside out, fold the top down 1" (1½") two times, so that the raw edge of the fabric is no longer showing.

5 Along the bottom edge of this fold, stitch the top seam down using a straight stitch.

6 Turn the bag right side out, and push out the corners so they are as square as possible.

7 Press down the bottom corners so that the side seams are flat against the center of the bottom of the backpack. Place one grommet 1½" from the point, in the center, on each side of the backpack. Follow the directions that come with the grommet setter.

8 Fold up the corners about 2½" and stitch in place against the side seams of the backpack.

9 Turn the bag inside out and sew using an overcast stitch, around the raw edges of the fabric along the side seams. This will keep the fabric from unraveling.

10 Turn the backpack right side out and again place grommets around the top of the bag, one in the center of the back and eight more spread evenly—approximately 2⅜" (3⅜")—around the top opening. When you put the strap in, you will see why it is important to have an odd number of grommets (nine) with one in the back center.

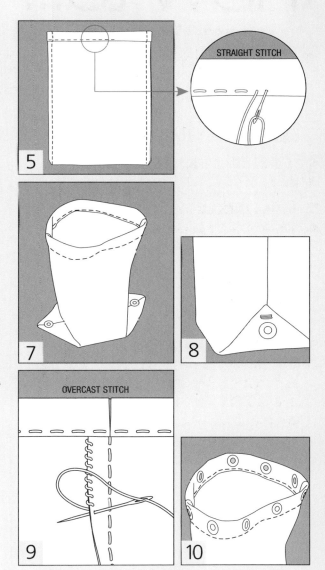

STRAIGHT STITCH

5

7

8

OVERCAST STITCH

9

10

how to...

11 Fold the strap in half and pin the center of the strap to inside center front of the backpack. Moving in opposite directions, weave each end through the grommet holes until both ends emerge together through the back center hole.

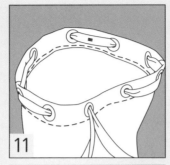

12 Thread the ends of the strap through the grommets on the bottom sides of the bag. Pin the end of each strap to the strap on the other side of the grommet. Pull the strap to close the top of the bag. Try it on; adjust the strap length to fit comfortably. Sew to secure, at the ends and at the top center.

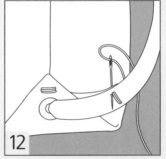

13 If you are using rope to make your straps, you can tie the ends in a fancy sailor knot to secure them.

    a. Pull one end of your strap through the grommet.

    b. Wrap that end three or four times loosely around the rope on the other side of the grommet.

    c. Thread the loose end through the loops and pull tight.

WARNING: If you are using mountain-climbing rope, it will unravel if you don't burn the ends with a lighter or match. Kids, please ask an adult to help.

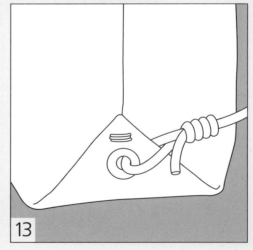

variations

Two-tone backpack: If you are feeling adventurous, you can also make a two-tone backpack—one with different material at the bottom.

a. Cut two pieces of fabric 11½" x 11½" (16" x 14½"). These will be the top pieces of the bag.

b. Cut one piece of fabric 11½" x 13" (16" x 15"); this will be the bottom of the bag.

c. Along the 11½" (16") side, pin one piece of the top fabric, right sides together, to either side of the bottom fabric. Sew a seam using the back stitch, ½" from the edge.

d. Sew using an overcast stitch around the raw edges of the seams so they won't unravel.

e. Now you have "one piece" of fabric. Follow directions on page 42 for making the backpack.

Bucket bag: Follow steps 1–9 for the backpack (no need for grommets in step 7). Also, you can skip step 8, turning up the corners, like Ellie did when she made this bag. Only put two grommets at the top of the bag—one on either side seam. Then, tie a single strap through the grommet holes; make sure it's long enough to go over your shoulder. Secure the straps as shown in step 12 or 13.

Sailor Totes

I love these bags. I have made quite a few: some are floppy (out of old beach towels) and some are stiff (out of heavy canvas and denim). They are incredibly useful. I use mine for grocery shopping, for collecting driftwood and shells at the beach, and for carrying around sewing or knitting projects; one tote is now permanently in use as the home for our set of driftwood building blocks. Of course you can just pack one up with your towel, sunscreen, and book, and head to the beach. Sailors used to make bags like these in which to carry large blocks of ice, and also to practice their sewing in the days when sails were hand sewn and ropes (or *lines*, as they are called in sailor lingo) handmade. You can make these bags on a sewing machine if you have one, but it's fun and good practice for kids to stitch by hand. Help them out with a few stitches here and there so they don't get discouraged. Take your bag to the beach and sew while your kids bury your feet in the sand.

If you want your bag to stand up on its own, you will need to use stiff, heavy canvas, blue jean material, or something similar. You may find it difficult to get your needle (either hand or machine) through the material, especially when you are sewing through several layers when adding the straps. A friend, a self-described former wardrobe girl in the movie business, shared this great trick: pound the seams a few times with a hammer; the needle will go through the layers more easily.

what you need

- Fabric…Heavy canvas or blue jean material will work well if you want the bag to stand up on its own. Otherwise, an old beach towel makes a nice floppy bag, replete with summer memories.

  Two sizes…For the small bag, you need a piece of fabric 20" x 30" for the bag, and a piece 3½" x 35" for the straps. For the large bag, you need a piece of fabric 26" x 42" for the bag, and a piece 4" x 48" for the straps.

- Measuring tape or ruler

- Scissors

- Chalk for marking

- Pins

- Heavy-duty needle…This is important; otherwise you won't be able to get your needle through the layers of canvas.

- Thread…Since a thick line of stitching is part of the design, I used a heavy crochet cotton (size 5), but you can use heavy cotton thread, or fine and not-too-stiff cotton twine.

- Thin rope or twine to reinforce the handles (optional)

how to...

...make a sailor tote

NOTE: Instructions are for the small size, with dimensions for the large size noted in parentheses. If you are using canvas, you can ignore the instructions about the right and wrong sides of the fabric because both sides are the same.

1 Cut a rectangle of fabric 20" x 30" for the small bag (26" x 42" for the large bag).

2 The dotted lines on the illustration at right show seams and folds. Draw them on your fabric with chalk.

3 Fold the rectangle in half, wrong sides together. With the fold on the bottom, lap the edges on both open sides 1" and pin. This means you overlap the two edges to make a seam, instead of just folding the material flat.

4 Turn under a small amount (about ⅛") of raw fabric edge and sew the outside of the lapped seams. For this bag, always sew straight stitches that are perpendicular to, and go across the seam.

5 When this is done on both sides, turn the bag inside out and sew the other sides of the lapped seams. Remember to turn the raw fabric edges under as you sew.

diagrams

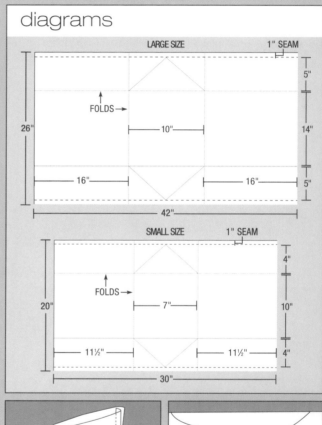

LARGE SIZE   1" SEAM

26"

FOLDS →

10"

5"

14"

16"

16"

5"

42"

SMALL SIZE   1" SEAM

20"

FOLDS →

7"

4"

10"

11½"

11½"

4"

30"

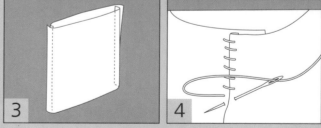

3

4

6 Turn the bag right side out again. Following the fold marks you drew on your fabric, fold the bag into a box-like shape with the corners folded down.

7 Turn up the triangle-shaped corners so they meet the side of the bag at the sewn side seams.

8 Sew along edges of the triangles to secure them to the sides of the bag; turn the bag inside out and sew the bottom of the triangle as well. Turn the bag right side out again.

9 Fold down the top seam 1½" all around, toward the inside of the bag. Pin in place.

10 Again turning under the raw edges, sew the top seam. Stitch as explained in step 4. Make sure the seam is on the inside of the bag.

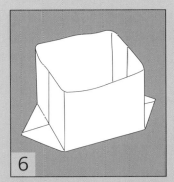

6

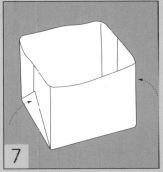

7

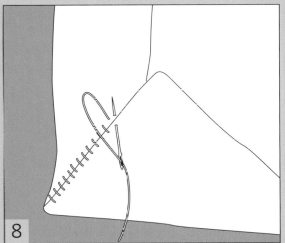

8

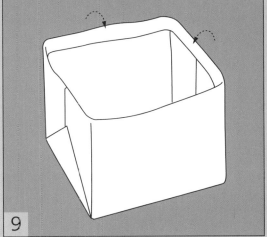

9

how to...

11 For the handles, cut two pieces of fabric 3½" wide x 35" long (4" wide x 48" long).

12 With the wrong side up, fold in the edges so they meet in the middle, making the straps 1¾" (2") wide. Pin them so they stay folded.

13 Starting at the center bottom of the bag and about 2" (3") in from the sides, pin the ends of the first strap to the bag.

14 As you pin down the strap, taper toward the top. The center of each strap will become a handle. Sew the strap to the bag.

15 Repeat steps 13–14 with the other strap. Steps 16–18 are optional. If you decide to skip them, fold the handle fabric toward the center again and stitch in place.

16 To reinforce the handle, sew a braid of rope on the inside. Cut 6 (9) pieces of rope, about 30" long each, and fold each piece in half. Knot a small piece of string around the fold.

17 Divide the 12 (18) strands into three sets, with 4 (6) strings each; braid until it is 4" (6") long. Knot at the end; trim loose ends to 2".

18 Place this braid at the underside center of the handle. Fold the handle again to cover the braid, and sew it closed, using a baseball stitch. Repeat steps 16–18 for the other strap.

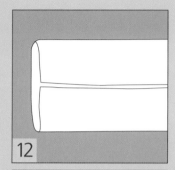

12

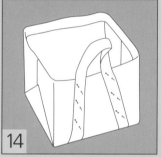

14

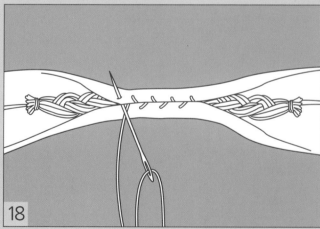

18

write some postcards...

Write some postcards. Everybody loves to get a postcard and they're fun to write and collect. Send them to your friends, your grandparents, your favorite teacher. Can't think of anything to say? Draw a picture. You can even make a game of it—send several postcards with different words to make one message!

Sometimes it's hard to find stamps, and the written postcards sit in your book until you get home. To avert this near tragedy, buy some postcard stamps before you leave. That is, if you are not traveling to a foreign country—in that case your postcard wouldn't go very far.

Remember to bring your address book on vacation!

Sarongs

Sarongs are incredibly useful at the beach. They are much less bulky than towels; a few in your backpack take up hardly any room and are as light as air. Or simply wrap one around your bicycle handlebars and take off. Sarongs are worn in many parts of the world, under many different names, by men and women alike. I like to wear one as a skirt over my bathing suit, take it off and sit on it on the sand, use it to dry off from my swim, and then wrap it around myself again for the walk home. I rarely bring a towel to the beach. For my kids I just bring a couple of extra sarongs. They like to use them to lie on the sand and wrap up after their swims.

Sarongs are easy to make from any kind of thin cotton and fun to dye, too. I like the idea of using natural dyes, so I used turmeric. My first attempt faded in the sun, so I was pretty fussy when I set up my turmeric dying, adding an overnight vinegar bath and a salt soak to the process. You may or may not know that turmeric is a spice used in Indian foods. The color is a beautiful golden yellow that will remind you of Indian marketplaces, and though it fades some with time, it continues to look great all summer long.

There are many ways to tie a sarong. To wear it as a skirt, wrap it around your waist once, or twice, as you like. Tie the corners into a knot. You can make a dress the same way; just start under your arms instead of at your waist.

what you need

Two sizes...Small measures 36" x 60" finished. Large measures 43" x 80" finished.

The sizes are, of course, not set in stone. If you are very tall, make the large one a bit wider, and so on. Wrap the fabric around yourself or your kids before cutting and hemming so you can see what works for you.

- Fabric (light fabrics such as muslin and Indian cotton work best, but even an old cotton sheet makes a nice sarong)

  For the small sarong, you need one piece of fabric measuring 37" x 61"

  For the large sarong, you need one piece of fabric measuring 44" x 81"

- Needle
- Thread

If you want to dye your cotton, you also need:

- Water
- A large pot
- Stove
- 2-ounce jar of turmeric
- 2½ cups of white vinegar (not used all at once)
- 1 cup of kosher salt

how to...

...make a sarong

1 If the fabric is new, wash and tumble dry it first. This will allow it to shrink and also will remove the sizing (a chemical put on fabric when it's made). This is an important step if you plan to dye the fabric, because the sizing may keep the dye from adhering.

2 Cut the fabric to the exact size you want: 37" x 61" for a small sarong or 44" x 81" for a large sarong.

3 Thread a needle. Using a running stitch, sew around all four sides of the sarong, folding the raw edge twice as you go, about ¼" per fold. When you are 2" from a corner, fold down a ¾" corner of the fabric. Continue to fold raw edges under twice and stitch as you round the corner. When you have finished, your folded seams will make a new corner.

NOTE: This sounds like a lot of sewing, but don't worry; this stitch goes quickly. Since the fabric is light, you can run the needle in and out of the fabric several times before pulling the thread through. Be careful not to pull it too tight, or your seam will pucker. An occasional back stitch (see page 42) will help keep your running stitch flat.

diagrams

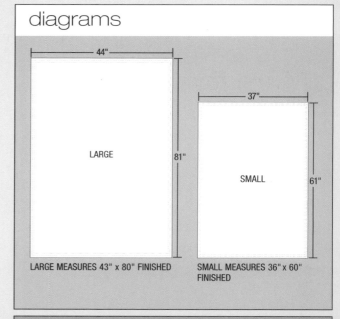

44"

LARGE

81"

37"

SMALL

61"

LARGE MEASURES 43" x 80" FINISHED

SMALL MEASURES 36" x 60" FINISHED

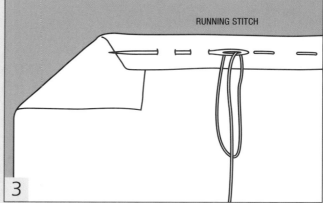

RUNNING STITCH

3

4 When you have finished hemming your sarong, you can dye the fabric in turmeric or decorate it with stitching (see embroidery stitches, page 90). Or just leave it alone, and wear it as is.

...dye the fabric

WARNING: The dye bath is scalding hot, so keep your kids away from the stove.

1 Start with a washed, dried, and hemmed sarong.

2 Put the sarong in a bowl of water, or in a stopped-up sink, and leave it to soak while you prepare the dye bath.

3 Place 1 gallon of water in a large pot on the stove.

4 Add the turmeric and ½ cup of the vinegar.

5 Wring the excess water from the sarong, and place it in the pot with the turmeric and vinegar.

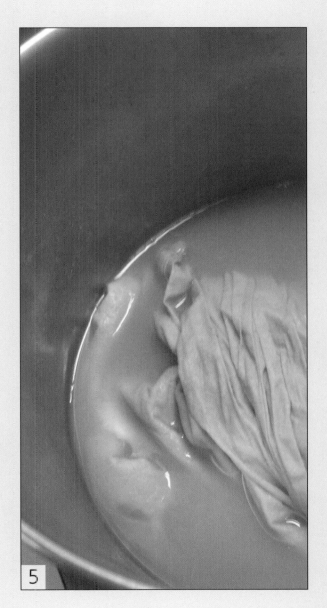

5

how to...

6 Simmer for 45 minutes to 1 hour, stirring and turning occasionally. The fabric gets heavy when it's wet, so be careful that you don't knock over the pot when agitating the fabric.

7 The color should be a strong, vibrant yellow. Remove the sarong from the pot and rinse it under warm running water.

8 Fill a large bowl with 12 cups of water, 2 cups of vinegar, and the sarong. Leave to soak overnight.

9 The next day, pull the sarong from the vinegar bath and wring out excess water, but *don't* rinse.

10 Fill a large bowl with water; mix in 1 cup of kosher salt and the sarong. Soak for ½ hour.

11 Wash and dry, separately for the first time so that no dye gets on your other clothes.

NOTE: It may seem fussy to soak the fabric twice, but the vinegar and salt baths will help to keep the color strong. It will fade with washing and exposure to the sun, but not as much as it would without those extra steps. Commercial cying is done with chemicals that help the color adhere to the fabric. Ours is a totally natural and safe dye bath. And the color is gorgeous.

Chessboards & Checkerboards

Let's face it, sometimes kids get antsy even at the beach. It's nice to have a game to play. If you are very clever and bring a beach umbrella with you, a game of checkers in the shade is a good way to get the kids to take a break from the sun. Our game board is portable and won't be damaged by a little water and sand. Make one, roll it up, and carry it to the beach. Before you settle down to play, search for rocks and shells to use as playing pieces (you can decorate them, too; see page 22). Play rocks versus shells, clamshells versus scallop shells, or design your own chess pieces—white and black pebbles for pawns, oyster shells for the queens, and so on.

This is a great project for small kids, new to sewing. With a little help, kids can cut their own felt squares and practice their stitches. Who cares if the felt squares are a little uneven and the checkerboard a bit askew? The finished board will be charming, and you will have created something else fun for you and your kids to do at the beach.

what you need

- Scissors
- Felt (a 12" square is exactly enough)
- Two pieces of canvas or other heavy cloth, 14" x 14"
- Pins
- Needle
- Embroidery thread (2 colors: 1 to match the felt, the other to match the canvas)
- Piece of fabric ribbon (24" long)
- 24 seashells or rocks for checkers or 32 for chess

how to...

...make a chessboard or checkerboard

1 Cut 32 squares (1½") of felt.

2 Pull a few threads from the sides of both pieces of the canvas so that they start to fringe just a bit.

3 Pin your felt squares to one of the pieces of canvas every 1½", leaving a 1" border all around. A chessboard or checkerboard is eight squares by eight squares, in two colors. Here the felt serves as one color, and the canvas the other.

4 Thread your needle with embroidery thread to match the felt, and sew each square in place with stitches around the edge. I like an X in each corner and one stitch in the center of each side.

5 Pin the second piece of canvas to the back of the checkerboard. It will cover the stitching on the underside of the board. Sew along the edge, approximately ½" in, using the running stitch (see page 60), with thread that matches the canvas color.

5

6 Fold a piece of 24-inch-long ribbon in half and stitch the center onto the underside of the board at a center edge. Roll up the board, tie the ribbon, and take it to the beach.

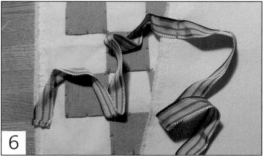

6

7 You can make your own checker or chess pieces (see page 22) or just find rocks and shells at the beach before you play.

7

Mermaid Dolls

I threw a sewing birthday party for my daughter when she turned five. Fifteen little girls, each wielding a needle, made stuffed dolls and bears out of felt. All my friends thought I'd lost my mind, but all the kids went home happy with a doll or bear of their own that they'd made themselves (with a little help here and there). Recently, my kids and I were listening to the fourth Harry Potter book on tape. During the part where Harry rescues Ron from the Merpeople in the lake, we were inspired to make a merfamily out of felt. Felt is a perfect sewing material for kids. It doesn't unravel, so you don't have to fold under any raw edges. It's easy for kids to make whatever they want. You can use our templates and make a mer-family. Or you can let your kids draw something—a sea monster, a starfish, their brother or sister—trace it on felt, and let them go. No shape is wrong, and I always say that when you are making monsters, the scarier the better. Before you stuff and sew your dolls together, decorate them with more felt or embroidery stitches.

I have a weakness for all-wool felt. Craft stores usually carry polyester and wool/rayon mixes, which also work well for this project, but wool felt is so soft and the colors so saturated that it's worth the extra expense.

what you need

- Scissors
- Templates (see page 158)
- Pins
- Felt
- Needle
- Embroidery thread
- Stuffing (Polyester or wool stuffing is available in craft and sewing stores, though in a pinch cotton balls from the drugstore work also.)
- Yarn or string for hair

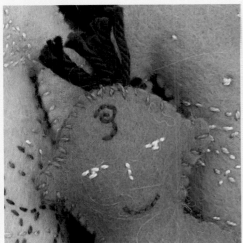

how to...

...make a mermaid doll

1 Enlarge a template (mermaid, merman, mergirl, or merbaby) following the directions on page 158. Cut it out. Now you have a pattern you can use to cut your felt.

2 Pin your pattern to the felt. Cut out two—a front and a back.

3 Thread a needle with embroidery thread and decorate the front of your doll (see page 90 for how to embroider). Using different colored threads, you can make a face and add scales to the tail. Anything goes: a tattoo on the arm, a beard for dad, a bikini top for mom and sis.

4 Pin the front and back pieces of the doll together. Using embroidery thread that matches your felt, start sewing around the edge using the overcast stitch. Keep your stitches fairly close together so the stuffing won't fall out.

5 Start to fill the doll with stuffing as you sew. I like to start sewing at the top of the head, stuffing the arms and tail and finally the body and head as I stitch around the doll. If you leave all the stuffing until the end, you will have a hard time reaching the tighter spots. This is the hardest part, and small kids will need help with this, especially with the arms. Use a pencil or a chopstick to push stuffing into places you can't reach with your fingers.

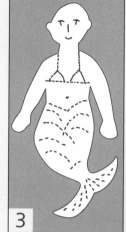

3

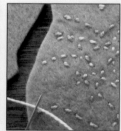

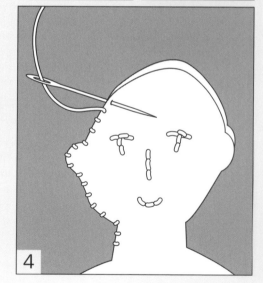

4

6 When the doll is completely stuffed and sewn, it's time to add hair. Using yarn or string, cut pieces twice as long as you would like the hair to be. Start by cutting twenty or thirty pieces, and cut more if you need it.

7 Take two pieces of the cut yarn and fold them in half. Now you have four strands of "hair." Using a color of embroidery thread that blends with the hair, make a stitch around the hair at the fold and through the top of the head. If you do a triple stitch at the beginning and end, you don't need to make a knot; just trim the excess string. Continue to move around the head, attaching four strands at a time until your merperson has a full head of hair.

8 Give your doll a haircut to get rid of any uneven ends.

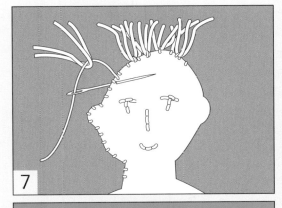

7

variations

I also included a template for a mermaid that mirrors the merman in shape. You can enlarge both of these templates to any size you like and make a set of pillows for your bed or beach house sofa.

For very small kids, you can pick one of the simpler templates—for instance, the baby—make it large, and punch small holes (with an ⅛" hole punch; you can find these at crafts stores) all around the edge. Give the little ones a dull needle and show them how to stitch in and out of the holes.

8

Sea Monkeys

I have been making sock monkeys for my children and their friends for a few years. Often, I use mismatched socks; these are my orphan monkeys. Every monkey gets a hand-knit sweater and seems to have a personality all its own. I spent awhile trying to make a mermaid out of a pair of socks, but I was never happy with the results. No matter what I did they still—oddly enough—looked like monkeys. So I gave in. Thus the sock sea monkey. Remember sea monkeys? Those little sea pets that arrived in the mail in some kind of suspended animation and came alive when you added water. It shouldn't be a surprise to you that those creatures weren't really monkeys, but little shrimp. Let's face it, they looked nothing like monkeys.

Buy a new pair of socks for this project, or just use a pair (or two) the kids have outgrown—preferably one without holes or blackened bottoms. We've made monkeys from my kids' old baby socks. It's an adorable way to recycle their baby clothes and remember how tiny their feet once were. One thing I've discovered is that sea monkeys look a little funny if you use socks with a long foot and a short cuff (the part that comes up your leg). A longer cuff makes an impressive fish tail—just what every sea monkey needs.

what you need

- Two socks…They can be a pair or not, used or new, but should be about the same size.
- Chalk for marking
- Needle
- Thread
- Stuffing
- Scissors
- Pins
- Small amount of felt for eyes
- Embroidery thread for decorating

how to...

...make a
sea monkey

As you can see from the diagrams, sock 1 makes the
sea monkey body and fish tail, and sock 2 is cut up to
make the arms, mouth, monkey tail, and ears.

1 Turn sock 1 inside out and flatten it out so the heel is
facing up (as pictured below).

2 Mark shaping for the sides of the tail and sew along these
lines, using the back stitch (see page 42).

3 Turn sock 1 right side out and fill with stuffing.

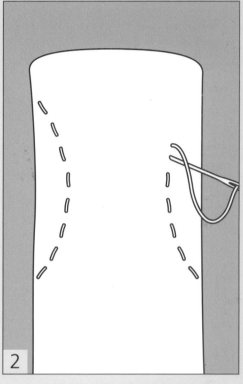

2

diagrams

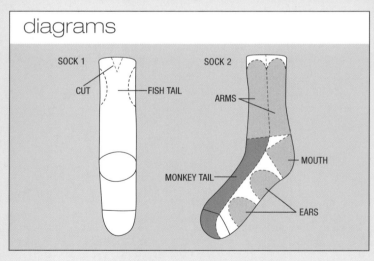

SOCK 1

CUT — FISH TAIL

SOCK 2

ARMS

MOUTH

MONKEY TAIL

EARS

4 Clip a small triangle out of the center of sock 1, at the top. Tuck in raw edges and sew the end closed into a fish tail shape.

5 Cut the heel from sock 2, and sew, turning under the raw edges, to sock 1 for the mouth. Fill with stuffing before you finish sewing around the mouth.

6 Cut arms from sock 2, turn under the raw edges and sew, tapering at the hand end.

7 Fill arms with stuffing and sew onto sock 1.

8 Cut the tail from sock 2, sew as you did the arms, but taper to a point at the end.

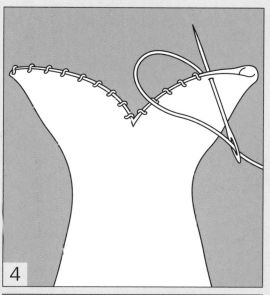

4

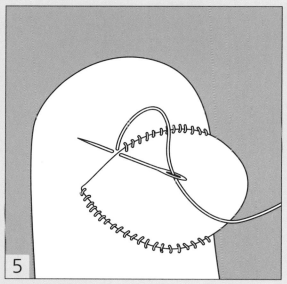

5

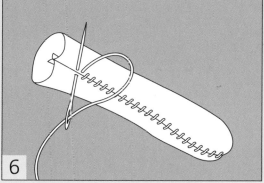

6

how to...

9 Stuff the monkey tail (on small monkeys the tail may not need stuffing) and sew to the backside of sock 1.

10 Cut ears from sock 2. Tuck in raw edges and sew around the half-circle tops. Sew the ears to the sides of the head.

11 Sew on felt circles for the eyes and embroider the mouth. When you are sewing on the eyes, it's a good idea to avoid having a knot that will show. Instead of knotting the end of your string, leave a 3- or 4-inch tail where the knot would be. When you are finished sewing, thread this tail onto your needle, push it through the body of the sea monkey, and trim off the excess.

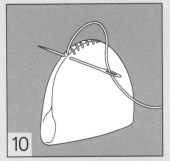

10

11

make some homemade lemonade...

Set up a stand and mix up a few pitchers of home-made lemonade, the quintessential childhood drink of summer. This sounds like a lot of lemonade, but you'll find it disappears fast.

LEMONADE

2 cups of sugar syrup (2 cups of water, 2 cups of sugar)
4 cups of lemon juice
12 cups of cold water

1. Make the sugar syrup by boiling the 2 cups of water and 2 cups of sugar just until the sugar has dissolved.
2. While the sugar syrup is cooling, squeeze lemons until you get 4 cups of juice.
3. Mix the sugar syrup and lemon juice into a large pitcher or thermos with the 12 cups of water.

Stitched Samplers

I like to bring a project with me nearly everywhere I go. I knit or sew while waiting for the school bus or for my editor to get off the phone, during my son's baseball games, at the dentist's office, and at children's birthday parties. A little bit of work here and there really adds up, and besides that, I can talk while I work. At a ten-year-old's party awhile back, I was embroidering a map of my favorite island with its black-and-white-striped lighthouse. I noticed that Claire, one of the party guests and apparently not in the mood for baseball, was standing over my shoulder watching me sew. After a few minutes, I offered her some canvas and thread. She's a very creative girl (see her seashell name collage on page 23) and she immediately started her own embroidery with her name and some daisies. Beautiful. I love to meet kids like Claire, kids who like to make things. I read somewhere—and it has bothered me since—that in the eighteenth century a child of eight could make better stitches, neater and smaller, than the average adult today can. I feel that with the proper encouragement, kids nowadays could find sewing every bit as engaging as video games.

Embroidery is really just sewing, but it intimidates many people. I was once one of those people. Books show incredibly complicated-looking projects with hundreds of intricate stitches—things that look like you could spend the rest of your life stitching, and still never finish. Then I realized that embroidery is just like drawing, but with a needle and thread on fabric. With the simplest straight stitch, you can create lines and shapes and words. When you get comfortable, add a couple more stitches. For me, the five stitches on page 90 are enough for you and your kids to make anything you want.

what you need

- Scissors
- Fabric…you can embroider on anything: cotton canvas, linen, denim, a pillowcase
- Chalk pencil
- Embroidery hoop (optional but a good idea, especially for thin fabrics)
- Embroidery needle (embroidery needles have slightly larger eyes so it's easier to thread them)
- Embroidery thread…I like DMC perle cotton size 8, but any embroidery thread will do.

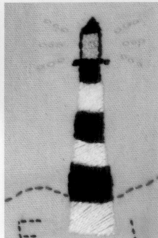

how to...

...embroider

Think about what you want to embroider. You may want to sew a beach scene, the shape of your favorite island, a poem about the sea, or the name of a special child. Of course, anything goes, and you can embroider the shapes of flowers, seashells, trees, people, surfboards, circles, stars, your house—whatever you can draw or write, you can sew.

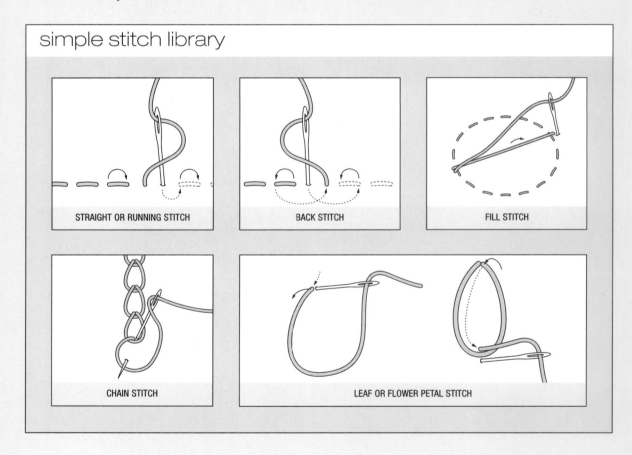

simple stitch library

STRAIGHT OR RUNNING STITCH

BACK STITCH

FILL STITCH

CHAIN STITCH

LEAF OR FLOWER PETAL STITCH

1 Cut a piece of fabric to whatever size you like. Remember to leave room for a border if you plan to frame it, or room for seams if you plan to make a pillow.

2 With a chalk pencil, lightly draw what you want to embroider. Start with the general shape; you can come back and add more detail later.

3 Pick a place to start and center the inside half of the embroidery hoop underneath it. Place the larger, adjustable half on top. Tighten the hoop and pull the material so it is held taut.

4 Thread a needle with a 12-inch-long piece of embroidery thread. Make a knot at the end and start to embroider using one of the stitches on the previous page.

5 Keep going, moving the embroidery hoop and changing colors as necessary until you are finished.

6 When you near the end of a thread, or want to change colors, bring the needle and thread to the back of the fabric and run under about 1" of stitches. Cut off any excess string. You don't need to tie a knot.

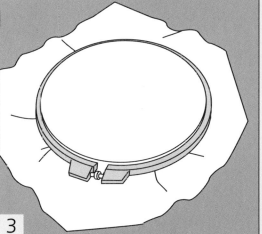

Memory Boxes

I got this idea indirectly from Gail's crafty friend, who lives in Europe and wrote a postcard from Provence saying that her daughter had a frog in her memory box. We jumped to the conclusion that the frog was dead and that her friend was letting her keep it in her box. We thought, what a great idea—a memory box to hold vacation treasures! Kids can decorate a box, take it on a trip, and use it to hold things that will remind them of their vacation…shells, rocks, starfish, ferry tickets, postcards.

We were thinking that a dead frog was one step too far, but were impressed that the friend, who's usually very tidy, let her daughter keep one in a box. What an adventurous and easygoing mother! Well, it may not surprise you that frog was alive, and the memory box was really a kind of terrarium where this smart woman's kids can keep small living creatures because they are not allowed pets. Personally, I was relieved to hear that the frog was alive.

what you need

- A box…I like cigar boxes because they are sturdy and a good size—cigar stores regularly get rid of extra boxes for a small fee. A shoebox or small shipping carton will work as well.
- Paint…poster or acrylic
- Paintbrush
- Mod-Podge or white craft glue (see page 18 for how to use glue as Mod-Podge)
- Trim…ribbon, ricrac (optional)
- Paper to cut for decorating
- Scissors
- White craft glue (optional)

how to...

...make a memory box

1 Decorate your box using paint, Mod-Podge (see page 20 for how-to tips), ribbon or ricrac until you are happy with it. Remember, Mod-Podge works best with smaller pieces of paper (otherwise the paper gets all wrinkly). If you want to cover part of your box with larger sheets (like we did with our box lined with bunny origami paper), just cut pieces to size and glue to the box.

2 When the box is dry, your kids can take it on your trip to fill with treasures…starfish, shells, postcards, or ferry tickets. Or they can just keep it on their desk or shelf, filled with colored pencils or erasers, stamps, or good luck charms. You'll want one, too.

Vacation Books

I always encourage my kids to write stories, and telling a vacation story is a good starting-off point. These are not to be confused with the dreary back-to-school "What I Did for the Summer" essays. This is a vacation story with photographs or drawings, bound like a real book: a keepsake! We had such a good time making the mermaid sculpture on the beach that I thought the whole story would make a great little book. Walker, eight years old, was a big help in the making of the mermaid, so I enlisted him to write about it. The finished book is adorable—Walker wrote a great story (and has very nice handwriting). We illustrated our book with photos, but kids can also draw pictures or make collages. In fact, a blank book like this would be a great vacation journal, for writing and drawing.

The binding is a variation on traditional Japanese bookbinding. It's simple—though it looks complicated, you'll see it's not when you try it—and the final book looks very professional. You can use colored thread, if you like, to liven up the outside and almost any color or kind of paper on the inside. This may be the beginning of a summertime publishing venture.

what you need

- Scissors
- Paper for covers…card stock, cardboard, or heavy art paper works well
- Paper for the pages…construction paper, copier paper, origami paper, vellum, or drawing paper—anything you like
- Bone folder for scoring paper (optional)
- Pencil
- Ruler
- ⅛ " hole punch (optional)
- Needle…one with a large eye
- String…I used size 5 crochet cotton, but you could also use embroidery thread, which is a bit finer, or twine from the hardware store.

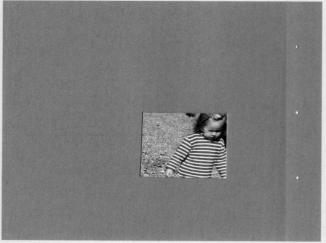

but her clay body

and her Tail

how to...

...make a vacation book

1 Cut the covers and all the pages for your book. We made ours 7½" tall x 9" wide. Use this size for your first book, and then when you get the hang of it you can make books any size you like. If you are writing a story, you may want to write on and illustrate the pages before binding the book.

2 Score the front cover and the inside pages (leave the back cover alone) along a straight line 1" from the edge you plan to stitch. Scoring means using a tool to press down on the paper, making an indented line that allows the paper to fold easily. When you fold the paper on the scored line, the fold is neat and crisp, with no creases. You can use a bone folder (especially made for this task and available at art stores) or a letter opener. The point of a ballpoint pen that is out of ink also works well for scoring the paper.

3 Mark holes for stitching. The holes should be placed every 1½" from top to bottom, and ¾" from the side edge. It's easy to mark your holes with a template: cut a piece of heavy paper to the same size as your book, and use a ruler to mark where the holes should go. Then, use a thick needle (or a small hole punch) to make your holes. Place this template over the pages for your book, a few at a time, and punch holes in all the pages.

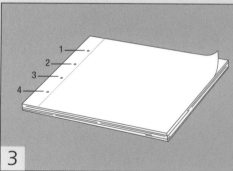

NOTE: The needle and string need to go through each hole three times, so don't make the holes too small. You might want to make a small test book first before binding any precious artwork. Also, for very young children, make the holes bigger by using a larger hole punch so they will have an easier time sewing the book together.

4 Thread a needle with your string and stack your pages so that the holes line up. If you are having trouble getting the holes to line up, put a needle through one of the holes a few pages at a time until the pages and the holes are aligned. It doesn't matter if the pages are not perfectly even the book will still look great.

5 Start sewing from the underside of your book. Go up through hole 3. Don't knot the end—we'll do that later—just leave a 4-inch tail hanging out the back.

6 Bring the needle and thread around the spine and up from the underside through hole 3 a second time.

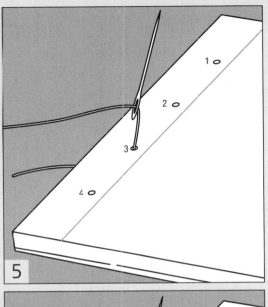

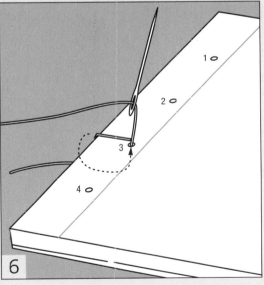

how to...

7 Sew across the top of the book and down through hole 4.

8 Sew around the spine and down through hole 4 a second time.

9 Sew around the bottom edge of the book, and from the top, go down through hole 4 for the third time.

10 From the underside, sew up through hole 3 for the third time.

11 Across the top, sew down through hole 2.

12 Sew around the spine and down through hole 2 a second time.

13 From the underside, sew up through hole 1.

14 Sew around the top edge and up through hole 1 a second time.

15 Sew around the spine and up through hole 1 a third time.

16 Across the top of the book, sew down through hole 2 for the third time—tie this end in a double knot with the original loose end. Trim ends to ½".

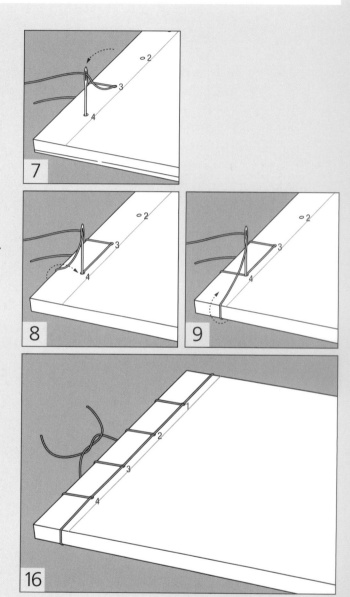

bake some homemade cookies...

You can even sell them at your lemonade stand. This is my favorite cookie recipe by far. The cookies are delicious: flat and crisp, just the way we like them. And they rate highly in our neighborhood cookie contest, judged by the kids, of course. The recipe was written by Kathleen King of Tate's Bake Shop when she was eleven years old. It appears in her new cookbook.

CHOCOLATE CHIP COOKIES*

Yield: 4 ½ dozen 3-inch cookies

INGREDIENTS

2 cups all-purpose flour
1 teaspoon baking soda
1 teaspoon salt
1 cup butter
¾ cup granulated sugar
¾ cup firmly packed dark-brown sugar
1 teaspoon water
1 teaspoon vanilla extract
2 eggs
2 cups semisweet chocolate chips

DIRECTIONS

1. Preheat oven to 350°F. Prepare greased cookie sheets.
2. In a large bowl, stir together flour, baking soda, and salt.
3. In another large bowl, cream butter and sugars. Add water and vanilla. Mix until just combined. Add eggs and mix lightly. Stir in the flour mixture. Fold in chocolate chips. Don't overmix.
4. Drop onto prepared cookie sheets using two tablespoons. Cookies will spread, so space them at least 2 inches apart.
5. Bake for 12 minutes, or until edges and center are brown. Remove cookies to a wire rack to cool.

Reprinted with permission from the Tate's Bake Shop Cookbook, St. Martin's Press

Bead &
Shell Necklaces

Stringing beads and shells is an ancient art and craft form, and a time-honored beach activity. We spent a lot of time this summer making necklaces, anklets, and belly chains, with and without shells. We added a few tricks—a wavy line of beads and a way to make a straight line of beading with small circles. By the end of the summer, there was no neck, ankle, or stomach unadorned. And we had a lot of fun doing it.

We set up our beading station on the deck by putting beads, separated by color, into little seashells. Needless to say, colors got mixed and shells got overturned—but it looked neat to begin with. I brought my own supply of glass seed beads in a rainbow of luminous colors. We also loved the tubes of glass beads available at the local five-and-dime. As the summer went on, and the stock there decreased, we eyed each other's beads jealously. We had the stock of remaining colors memorized, and tried to purchase politely, buying no more than we could use. The dwindling stock of black beads, though, did cause a run on them. You don't have to stick to the tiny glass beads; any size and shape of bead will do. It's fun to make your own from one of those bake-in-the-oven clays (such as Sculpey®). Remember to make the holes first (poke through the clay bead with a sewing needle or pin). After you bake the clay beads, it's too late.

what you need

- Beads
- Fishing line (easy to find in stores near the beach)
- Scissors
- Seashells, or pieces of shells, with holes in them

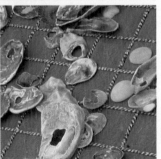

how to...

...bead

I don't think I really need to teach anyone how to make a bead necklace, but I did want to share some tricks we figured out when we were in our heavy beading phase. You can buy clasps at a craft or beading store, but I like the transient quality of beach beading—your creations are stuck on your body until they fall off.

TRIPLE KNOT. I find with fishing line that a double knot is just plain unreliable, but a triple knot really stays knotted.

SHELL AND BEAD NECKLACE. Find a beautiful shell, or piece of shell, with a hole in it. Fold your fishing line in the center, and thread the fold through the hole, creating a loop. Pull the loose ends through the loop. This helps the shell lie flat and in the center of your necklace. Add beads from both ends. Triple knot the ends to secure.

SECURE FIRST AND LAST BEAD. Start and end your beading by threading the fishing line through the first and last bead a second time. This way, if your knot breaks, the beads won't go flying. We learned this the hard way when Ellie's long belly chain broke when she was almost finished. Much crying and scrambling around the deck in search of tiny, rolling beads ensued.

MAKE A BELLY CHAIN. A long string of beads tied around your waist (really just above your hip bones) looks great with a two piece bathing suit and is a comfort in the cold winter months. Small beads work best; larger beads pinch your skin.

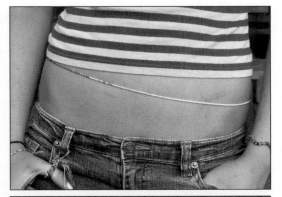

DO SOME WAVY BEADING. Put an odd number of beads onto your fishing line (7 or 9 work well). Bring fishing line around to the beginning and through the beads again. Pull the fishing line so the beads make a half circle. Repeat. You will see that this naturally sets up a wave pattern. It works best for chokers, bracelets, or anklets, or for hanging shells on a mobile, as the pattern stays best when it is pulled taut. This also works with beading string, if you have any.

BEAD SOME CIRCLES. The method is similar to that of wavy beading, above, but start with an even number of beads (8 or 10 work well) on your fishing line. Thread the fishing line through the first half of the beads. Pull the fishing line until the beads make a circle. Straight beading in between the circles looks great.

Friendship Bracelets

My daughter Ellie taught me everything (well, almost everything) I know about making friendship bracelets. Alas, not everyone can spend the entire summer at the seashore, so Ellie got her early training in friendship bracelets at the magical summer camp my kids have attended since they were three. At their camp, kids can do whatever they want all day long. And if, one morning, all they want to do is make friendship bracelets, that's fine. The camp has lots of young kids so they use the method of starting beginners on pieces of cardboard (see page 118). This helps the little ones keep the strings straight. I've seen four-year-olds making quite beautiful bracelets. Friendship bracelets are fun and pretty quick to make, so you can make a bunch and give them to—well, your friends. I know when summer is over because that's when I want to cut off (or untie) my friendship bracelets, or anklets, as the case may be. What looks great in the summer feels funny under a pair of socks. For me, this is the first sign of autumn, long before any leaves start to fall.

When you and your kids get the hang of making bracelets, you can always add more strings and make a wider bracelet, or double up two strings to make one knot and make a bulkier one.

Here are instructions for four different bracelets (my favorites)—chain, rainbow, V, and diamond. They build on each other, so it's good to start at the beginning and work your way up.

what you need

- Embroidery thread in different colors...I like using perle cotton in size 5 or size 3 (two brands are DMC and Anchor). You can find it at craft or needlepoint stores. This kind of thread is twisted, slightly shiny, and comes in tons of colors. You can also use traditional embroidery thread.

- Scissors

- Measuring tape or ruler

- Clipboard, safety pin, masking tape, or a piece of heavy cardboard

NOTE: You need something to hold the bracelet in place while you are working. Place the top knot under the clip on a clipboard, secure to a table with a piece of masking tape, or put a safety pin through the top knot and attach it to the knee of your jeans (I like this way best). If you are a beginner, you may want to work at first on a piece of cardboard (see page 118).

how to...

...make friendship bracelets

The string numbers in the instructions refer to the position of the string, not the actual string itself. As you make your knots, strings will change their numbers as they move across the bracelet. All the bracelets here are made with these two basic knots:

FORWARD KNOT (FK)

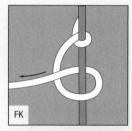

1 Cross the left-hand string over the string on its right, leaving a loop to the left—think of making the number 4 with your strings.

2 Wrap the left-hand string around and under the right-hand string. Bring the end up through the loop. Pull taut to make a knot. Hold the right-hand string firmly while knotting.

3 Repeat steps 1–2. This makes a double knot, which equals one FK.

BACK KNOT (BK)

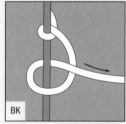

The back knot is exactly the same, but reversed.

1 Cross the right-hand string over the string to its left, leaving a loop to the right. This makes a backward number 4.

2 Wrap the right-hand string around and under the left-hand string. Bring the end up though the loop. Pull taut to make a knot. Hold the left-hand string firmly while knotting.

3 Repeat steps 1–2. This makes a double knot, which equals one BK.

for beginners

Cut four strings, 30" each. Knot them together at one end. Take a piece of heavy cardboard (about 5" x 8") and make a slit in the top and four slits on the bottom. Place the knot in the top slit, and the four strings in the bottom ones. The slits will keep the strings in order and hold the strings taut while you are knotting. To start working, remove string 1 from the cardboard; FK across strings 2, 3, and 4. On the bottom of the cardboard, move each string one space to the left, making room for the string now on the right (this keeps the strings straight). Keep making FK's and you will make the rainbow bracelet on page 120.

CHAIN BRACELET

This bracelet reminds me of the paper chains we used to make as kids. The knots are the same as above, but single, not double. If you like, cut four strings—two of each color—for a thicker bracelet.

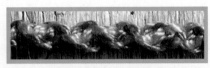

1 Cut two pieces of string (I used two different colors), 50" long each. Fold strings in half and make a knot at the fold, leaving a small loop at the top.

You will now have four strings to work with.

2 Separate the colors.

3 Grab the two strings of the color to the left and knot them (this is just like the FK, but you only knot once, not twice) over the strings of the other color. Pull snug.

4 Now grab the two strings of the other color, and knot them (this is just like the BK, but you only knot once, not twice) over the first. Pull snug.

5 Repeat until it's long enough.

6 To tie off: thread one half of your loose end strings through the loop at the start of your bracelet. Tie in a double knot with the rest of the loose strings. Trim ends to about 1"

how to...

RAINBOW BRACELET

This bracelet is fairly simple and uses only the forward knot (FK). It's a good idea to master this bracelet before trying the V or the diamond bracelets. If you've never made a friendship bracelet before, try one using the instructions for beginners on page 118.

1 Cut four pieces of string (I used four different colors), 60" long each. Fold strings in half and make a knot at the fold, leaving a small loop at the top.

2 You will have two strings of each color. I put the two colors next to each other for a thick stripe, but you can separate them for thinner stripes. The order in which you put your strings now will create the stripe order.

3 Start from the left, and FK string 1 over string 2. **REMEMBER TO DOUBLE KNOT.**

4 FK same string over string 3.

5 Continue to FK the same string over strings 4, 5, 6, 7, and 8. When you are finished with this first row (or stripe), that first string will have changed position and become string 8.

6 Start on the left again, and repeat steps 3–5 until the bracelet is long enough.

7 Tie off (see step 6 of the chain bracelet).

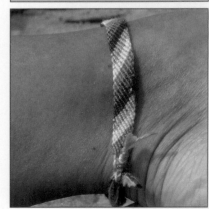

V BRACELET

This bracelet is similar to the rainbow bracelet, but the V uses both the FK over the left-hand strings and the BK over the right-hand strings. They meet in the middle, and another FK makes the point of the V.

1 Cut four strings, each 60" long, fold in half, and make a knot at the fold, leaving a small loop at the top. Now you have eight strings. Arrange the strings so that the left-hand 4 strings and the right-hand 4 strings are mirror images of each other (i.e., if a blue strings is string 1, it should also be string 8, and so on).

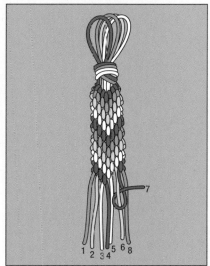

2 Start from the left, and FK string 1 over strings 2, 3, and 4. This is just like the beginning of the rainbow bracelet.
REMEMBER TO DOUBLE KNOT.

3 Now start from the right, and BK string 8 over strings 7, 6, and 5.

4 FK the two center strings (4 and 5) together.

5 Repeat steps 2–4 until the bracelet is the right length.

6 Tie off (see step 6 of the chain bracelet).

how to...

DIAMOND BRACELET

The diamond bracelet, which is trickier than previous bracelets, uses the FK and the BK. Follow the instructions on page 123 and refer to the chart below for details on how to make each part. Try to master the V bracelet before doing this one.

make the parts

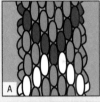

A. HOW TO MAKE THE V (WORK WITH COLOR B ONLY)

1. Start as you did with the the V bracelet. FK string 1 over strings 2, 3, and 4.

2. BK string 8 over strings 7, 6 and 5.

3. FK the center strings together.

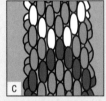

B. HOW TO MAKE THE SIDE TRIANGLES (WORK WITH COLOR A ONLY)

1. FK string 1 over strings 2 and 3.

2. FK string 1 over string 2.

3. BK string 8 over strings 7 and 6.

4. BK string 8 over string 7.

C. HOW TO MAKE THE UPSIDE DOWN V (WORK WITH COLOR B ONLY)

1. With color B in the center, FK the two center strings together.

2. BK string 4 over strings 3, 2, and 1.

3. FK string 5 over strings 6, 7, and 8.

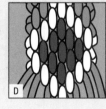

D. HOW TO MAKE THE CENTER OF THE DIAMOND (WORK WITH COLOR A ONLY)

1. FK the two center strings (4 and 5) together.

2. FK string 5 over strings 6 and 7.

3. BK string 4 over strings 3 and 2.

4. FK the center strings again.

5. FK string 5 over string 6.

6. BK string 4 over string 3.

7. FK the center strings again.

MAKE THE DIAMOND BRACELET

1 Cut three pieces of one color, each 60" long (this will be color A and is the background color) and one piece of a second color, 80" long (this will be color B and is the color of the diamonds).

2 Fold the four strings in half and knot; now you have eight strings. Arrange the strings so that the color B strings are in the center.

3 Start as you did with the V bracelet. FK string 1 over strings 2, 3, and 4. **REMEMBER TO DOUBLE KNOT.**

4 BK string 8 over strings 7, 6, and 5.

5 FK the center strings (4 and 5) together.

6 Repeat steps 3–5 two times. When you have done this, color B should be on the outsides.

7 Make the V.

8 Make the side triangles.

9 Make the upside-down V.

10 Make the center of the diamond.

11 Repeat steps 7–10 until the bracelet is long enough.

12 Tie off (see step 6 of the chain bracelet).

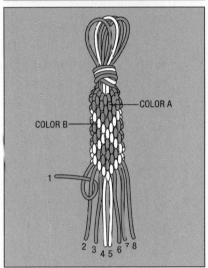

Macrame Bracelets

I was thinking about rope and string and bracelets a lot when a friend came home from a summer visit to her mom's lake house with two balls of vintage macrame string—red and navy blue. Remember macrame? It was a seventies thing. When I look at these bracelets, it brings me back to being twelve again…not a bad age from my current vantage point. This friend says she learned how to macrame plant hangers at a summer camp where they'd sing the Cat Stevens classic "Morning Has Broken" at the start of every camp day. Those were the days! The bracelets we made with her vintage string are some of my favorites. Look around your house, or perhaps around your mother's house, and see what you can find.

Another good thing, perhaps my favorite, about macrame bracelets, is that boys like them too. I was thrilled when my son, Ike, decided he wanted to make one. The bracelets are quite manly, and when they aren't reminding me of Huckapoo shirts and Bee Gees music on the radio, they remind me of old-time sailors sitting on deck making things with rope.

Since macrame bracelets are made by knotting the outer strings over the center ones, it helps to secure the center strings while you are working. Use a clipboard: Place your top knot under the clip and clamp the shorter, center pieces with another clip or a piece of tape. You'll see that we start the bracelets with the center threads shorter than the outer ones—since they don't do any of the knotting work, they don't need to be very long. If you don't have a clipboard, you can safety pin the top knot and the bottoms of the center strings to your jeans, or you can just tape them to a table.

what you need

- String…You can use pretty much any kind of string for these bracelets—embroidery thread, hemp string, cotton twine, or rope. Some of my favorite bracelets were made from a ball of polished cotton twine I bought at my local hardware store.

- Scissors

- Measuring tape or ruler

- Clipboard, tape, or safety pins

- Beads (optional)

how to...

...make macrame bracelets

Here are the two basic knots you will need for these bracelets:

LEFT KNOT

1 Bring the left-hand string over the two center strings; leave it slack to create a loop to the left. Think about making the number 4 with your strings.

2 Place the right-hand string over the left-hand string, under the two center strings, and up through the loop to the left. Pull both strings tight.

RIGHT KNOT

1 Bring the right-hand string over the two center strings; leave it slack to create a loop to the right.

2 Place the left-hand string over the right-hand string, under the two center strings, and up through the loop to the right. Pull both strings tight.

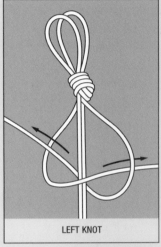

LEFT KNOT

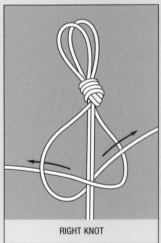

RIGHT KNOT

TWISTED COBRA BRACELET

This bracelet is very simple, using only one knot from the left (the left knot).

1 Cut two pieces of string, each 60" long. Fold string so that one side measures 15" and the other 45". Make a knot at the fold, leaving a small loop at the top. The 15" strings are the center pieces, and the 45" strings become the outside pieces.

2 Make a left knot.

3 Repeat left knots until the bracelet is long enough, and then tie off (see step 6 of the chain bracelet, page 119).

TWISTED COBRA

how to...

SQUARE KNOT BRACELET

This bracelet uses both the left knot and the right knot. If you lose track of whether it's time for a left knot or a right knot, look at the side loops and start on the same side as the last one.

1 Cut two pieces of string, each 60" long. Fold so that one side measures 15" and the other 45". Make a knot at the fold, leaving a small loop at the top. Again, the 15" strings are the center pieces.

2 Make a left knot.

3 Make a right knot.

4 Repeat steps 2–3 until your bracelet is long enough, and then tie off (see step 6 of the chain bracelet, page 119).

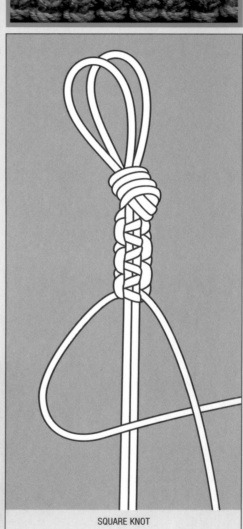

SQUARE KNOT

variation

Add beads to your macrame bracelets, if you like. Both the square knot and the twisted cobra bracelet look great with beads threaded over the two center strings. Place the bead and continue to knot as usual. You need beads with a large hole (I used African trading beads) if you want to thread them over the two center strings. Smaller beads look great threaded on the outside string of the twisted cobra bracelet. I think the one we made looks like a strand of DNA. I wonder if it would work for a science project?

write some poetry...

Memorize a poem about the summertime, or better yet, write one of your own about your summer vacation. Here's a poem by my son Ike and another by his friend Nikolai, both age ten and both big fans of the summer:

FLIPPING OVER

By Nikolai Stern

The water moving fast
Water in my eyes

With my friend that I never see
Sitting down flipping over
I see the fish underwater.

FIRE ISLAND

By Ike Kitman

Wearing no shoes
Biking with no helmet
Walking where no cars are allowed
On Fire Island

In the salty water boogie boarding
Getting hit hard by a wave so that
My stomach scrapes the sand
On Fire Island

Biking from Lonelyville to Fair Harbor
The wind in my face
Wanting some delicious ice cream
On Fire Island

Driftwood Building Blocks

I'd seen expensive building blocks made from tree limbs at a friend's house and thought, why not driftwood? I enlisted the help of my intrepid friend Susan to operate the power tools. A chop saw is definitely not a child's toy, especially when cutting uneven pieces of wood like driftwood, so I recommend that kids collect the driftwood, tell a handy parent or adult friend how they want it cut (*handy* being the operative word), and then scram. Or you can supervise an older child using a handheld saw, though this will obviously take longer.

The shapes you get will depend on what kind of wood you can find. I found a great haul of driftwood on a sandy beach with lots of smooth stones when I was learning how to make hot rocks. Not all beaches have driftwood, so collect it when you see it. It's a good idea to make a few blocks in each size (we made at least four, and sometimes more) so your structures will balance. A set of these blocks makes a great gift (packed in the small sailor tote) for anyone old enough not to try eating the pieces. Once the blocks are cut, the kids can get involved again by sanding the rough edges. Your friends will think you are amazing or crazy—but either way your kids will have cool, one-of-a-kind blocks to play with that will always remind them of their summer holiday. I like to think they retain their smell of the sea.

what you need

- Driftwood
- Marker or pencil
- Chop saw or handheld saw
- Sandpaper

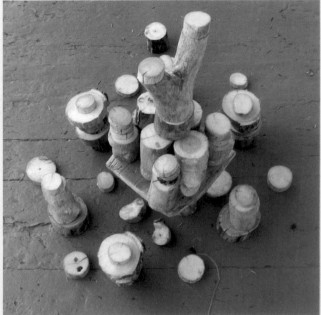

how to...

...make driftwood building blocks

WARNING: Cutting uneven pieces of wood, like driftwood, with a power tool is a dangerous business, and the use of a chop saw for this project is recommended only for people with experience using this tool.

1 Collect driftwood.

2 Look over your pile of driftwood and pick out pieces with promising Y joints, as pictured. This is where the tree limbs forked. Those pieces seem to be harder to find, so you should cut the Y's first.

3 Mark the wood where you want your first cuts. Be sure to keep all your cut lines parallel so your blocks will stand and stack.

4 Start cutting your pieces. Cut several of each size piece so you can make nice, balanced structures. Remember that some of the wood will end up as sawdust, so you need to measure and mark your cuts one at a time.

5 It's a good idea to make lots of the small pancake-shaped pieces. They are good for making tall towers.

6 When you have as many pieces as you want for your set, take some medium-grit sandpaper and sand the rough edges so they are smooth and the edges are slightly rounded.

7 If you are giving these driftwood blocks as a gift, consider making one of the small sailor totes to hold the blocks.

Toy Boats

What's a day at the shore without some toy boats? I was inspired for this project by a friend's collection of vintage wooden pond boats. They were handmade toys of another era, painted in nautical reds and blues, some with wheels so they could "float" across the floor, and all charming.

When I started this project, I didn't know much about boats and what makes them float and sail. I learned that a keel keeps a sailboat from tipping over, that there are many different kinds of sails, and that kids love to make and paint boats.

A nautical friend shared her knowledge of sail shapes. If I followed her directions well, we have a lateen rig (as on Sunfish boats), a gaff rig (as on a cat boat), and a square sail (as on a Viking vessel). And again I enlisted the help of my power-tool-wielding friend, Susan. She is very handy, and the wood we used, cedar deck planking, was left over from her deck project. The boats were fun to make, and not as difficult as I expected. They even float. And making the sails might even get some reluctant little boys interested in sewing.

what you need

- Templates for the boat shapes (see page 156)
- Wood...We used cedar 1″ x 6″ planks, but you can use other wood if you have some extra pieces lying around.
- Pencil or marker
- Jigsaw (jigsaws are dangerous, and if you are a kid reading this, we insist that you have an adult cut the boat shapes.)
- Sandpaper
- Exterior wood glue
- Hammer
- Small nails (I used 1¼″ brads)
- Masking tape (optional)
- Paint (I used acrylic latex enamel, available at hardware stores in 8-ounce cans) and paintbrush

PLUS THESE THINGS FOR THE SAILBOAT:

- Templates for the sails (see page 157)
- Twigs for the masts and sails:

  For the lateen rig: 1 twig for the mast, about 10½″ long, and 2 thinner twigs, about 9″ long

  For the gaff rig: 1 forked twig for the mast, about 10½″ long, and 1 thinner twig, about 8″ long

  For the square rig: 1 twig for the mast, about 10½″ long, and 1 thinner twig, about 8″ long

- Drill
- Fabric...anything will do, though it's probably better for the balance of the boat if the fabric is not too heavy

- Needle
- Thread
- Small (³⁄₁₆″) grommets and grommet setter (optional)
- Twine or heavy thread
- Two small screw eyes (for square rig sail boat only)

PLUS THESE THINGS FOR THE POND BOAT:

- ⅞″ dowel (for smokestacks on the pond boat)
- Nail set and wax furniture pencil (optional)

how to...

...make a sailboat

WARNING: Again, power tools are dangerous. The use of a jigsaw in this project is recommended only for people with experience using this tool.

1 Enlarge the two templates for the boat top and the keel of the sailboat onto a sheet of paper, following the directions on page 156. Cut out the shapes, place them on top of the wood, and trace them with pencil or marker.

2 With the jigsaw, cut out the two shapes from the wood.

3 Sand the cut sides, rounding all sharp corners, until the boat shapes are smooth.

4 The smaller shape goes on the bottom, to act as a keel and help keep the boat from tipping over. Glue the two shapes together, centering the keel under the boat top.

5 When the glue has set for a few minutes, hammer a couple of nails into the small piece. The nails should be long enough (I used 1¼" brads) to go through the small piece and into, but not through, the larger piece. They will act as clamps, helping to keep the wood pieces tightly together until the glue dries.

6 While you are waiting for the glue to set, decide what kind of sail you want. For the lateen rig or the gaff rig: enlarge the template for the sail, pin it to a piece of fabric, and cut out the sail. For the square rig, cut an 8" square piece of fabric.

7 Using the running stitch (see Sarongs, page 60), sew a hem around the outside of the sail, rolling the raw edges under twice, about ⅛" per turn, as you sew.

7

GAFF RIG

SQUARE RIG

LATEEN RIG

how to...

(HOW TO MAKE A SAILBOAT...CONTINUED)

8 If you have, or can find, some small grommets, they will give the sails an authentic look. Place them around the edges of the sails as shown on the templates. The square rig needs grommets just along the top, and one at each bottom corner.

9 Thread a needle with heavy thread and sew the sail to the thinner twigs and the mast, as shown. Sew through the grommets if you have them, or just through the fabric if you don't.

10 Mark the spot where you will place your mast. For the lateen rig, mark a spot in the center and 2¼" from the front. For the gaff rig, mark a spot in the center and 1½" from the front. For the square rig, mark a spot in the center and 4" from the front.

11 Drill a small hole the width of the bottom of your twig mast, and about ½" deep, into the top of the boat.

12 Before attaching the mast, paint your boat. The two layers can be different colors, if you like. Use masking tape to protect the layer you aren't painting, or just be careful.

13 When the paint is dry, put a small amount of wood glue into the hole you made for the mast, and place the mast, with the sail attached, into the hole. Let dry completely before trying to sail.

14 If you are making the square rig, screw two screw eyes into the wood (near the edges, approximately 3" from the back of the boat). Tie a small piece of string to each corner of the square sail, and attach the ends to the screw eyes.

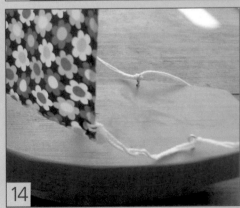

how to...

...make a pond boat

Feel free to mix and match, using all or part of the pattern. As for decorating, anything goes. Ike made a stealth graffiti boat (he used permanent markers for the writing) that he called *The Mom*.

WARNING: Power tools are dangerous. The use of a jigsaw in this project is recommended only for people with experience using this tool.

1 Enlarge the three templates for the pond boat onto a sheet of paper, following the directions on page 156. Cut out the shapes, place them on top of your wood, and trace them with pencil or marker.

2 With a jigsaw, cut out the three shapes from the wood.

3 With a jigsaw, cut two smokestacks from the dowel. We cut ours at a 45-degree angle, but you can make them straight, if you like.

4 Sand the cut sides, rounding all sharp corners, until the boat shapes and the dowels are smooth.

5 Place the smaller boat-shaped piece on top of the larger one. Glue in place.

6 When the glue has set for a few minutes, hammer a couple of nails into the small piece. The nails should be long enough (I used 1¼" brads) to go through the small piece and into, but not through, the larger piece. They will act as clamps, helping to keep the wood pieces tightly together until the glue dries.

7

7 Glue the rectangular top shape to the center of the smaller boat shape, and hammer nails to secure wood as you did above.

10

8 If you like, use a nail set to sink just a bit below the surface of the wood any nail heads that show. Fill in the hole using a wax furniture pencil. This is optional but will give you a smoother surface when you paint. You now have a three-tiered boat.

9 Glue on the smokestacks. Hold them in place for several minutes, until the glue starts to set a bit. Be careful of these smokestacks, as they are not attached as securely as the layers. Let the glue dry completely.

10 Paint your boat. The layers can be different colors if you like. Use masking tape to protect the layers you aren't painting—or, just be careful.

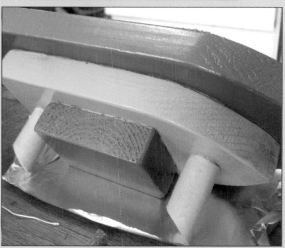

Backgammon Board

This backgammon board was designed by my friend Blake. In fact, Blake, a furniture designer in real life, known in the industry as the "King of Clean," gave me the idea for this book. On vacation, a pile of discarded snow fencing struck him as perfect for the alternating stripes on a backgammon board. He made one, and then showed everyone else how to make their own. I think four more were made in the space of a week. The red fencing is older, at least on this beach, and was hard to find. A search ensued, and people jealously guarded their piles of slats.

Don't worry if you can't find two colors of discarded snow fencing; in fact, don't worry if you can't find snow fencing at all. The slats in snow fencing are called laths and are available at lumberyards, and paint solves the problem of the color. If you buy new laths, but want an aged-looking board like ours, you can leave the boards outside for a bit and rough up the surfaces with sandpaper. Even when you're not playing backgammon, this board will look great on your coffee table. And maybe, if you're lucky, the kids will play game after game while you immerse yourself in your vacation reading.

what you need

Snow fencing (lath strips) varies in width, so you will figure out the exact dimensions of the pieces needed below as you go along.

- Discarded snow fencing or laths bought new from a lumber yard to make:

    Board strips…24 pieces approximately 7–7½" each (snow fencing is generally 4' long so you will get about 6 pieces from each board)

    Side frames…4 pieces

    Trim strips…2 pieces

- Center divider…1 piece of wood, about ¾" thick
- Backboard (¾" thick plywood or solid wood)
- Miter box (optional)
- Small handsaw
- ¾" Brads
- Hammer
- 30 rocks separated into two colors
- Dice

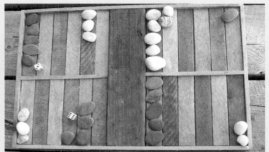

how to...

...make a
backgammon board

1 Collect discarded natural and red snow fence or buy laths at your local lumberyard.

2 Cut 12 pieces of each color to desired length (7–7½" works well). Using a miter box will ensure square cuts and a more finished look.

3 Find a piece of weathered ¾" thick wood to use as center divider. The width should be in proportion to the rest of the board but does not have to be a specific size.

4 Make the backboard: Lath strips range in width from around 1¼" to 1⅜". Because of this inconsistency, you must lay out the strips and the center divider to determine the length of the backboard. Placing two board strips end to end will determine the width of your backboard.

5 Find a piece of ¾" thick material (either plywood or solid wood) and cut to the dimensions determined in step 4. This will be the backboard, to which all the parts will be nailed. Also, cut the center divider so its length matches the width of the backboard.

6 Lay out your board strips, alternating colors, with six pieces on each side of the center divider. Start attaching the strips to the backboard by laying one strip flush along the edge and corner of the backboard and nailing through the face of the strip in two places about ¾" from each end. Butting one strip along the side of the next, nail each strip in place, stopping after attaching all the strips for one half of the

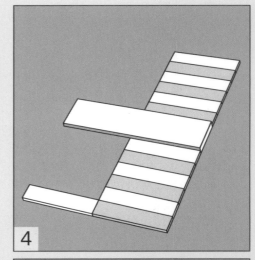

4

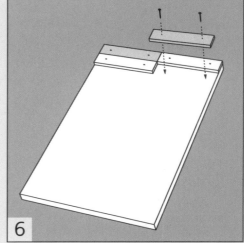

6

board. Nail the center divider in place and attach the strips on the other side.

7 After attaching all the board strips and center divider to the face of the backboard, cut and attach the side strips that will frame the board. Cut the strips for the short sides first. Cut the short sides the same width as the backboard. Attach them by nailing into the edge of the backboard. The strips will stick up above the face of the board about ¼", which will help keep the stones on the board. Measure the long side with the short-side strips in place, and cut the long strips to this length. If you are using a miter box you can also miter the corners for a more finished look.

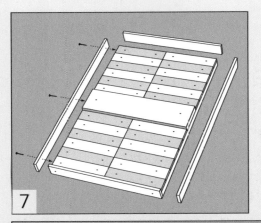

8 This last building step is optional. Cut a long ¼" strip from the edge of a piece of lath to use as trim to cover the area where the board strips meet along the center of the board. This piece of trim will also help stop the stones from passing the center of the board. Measure the distance from the inside of the side frame to the edge of the center divider and cut your trim strip to fit, then nail in place, covering the line created by the meeting of the board strips.

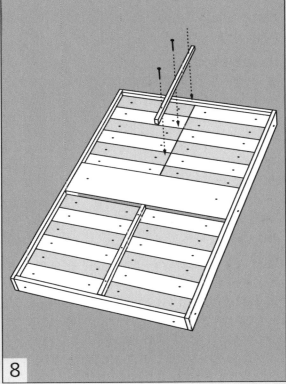

9 Collect 30 rocks: 15 in a dark shade and 15 in a light. Round flat rocks around 1" in diameter will work best. If you like, you can decorate the rocks.

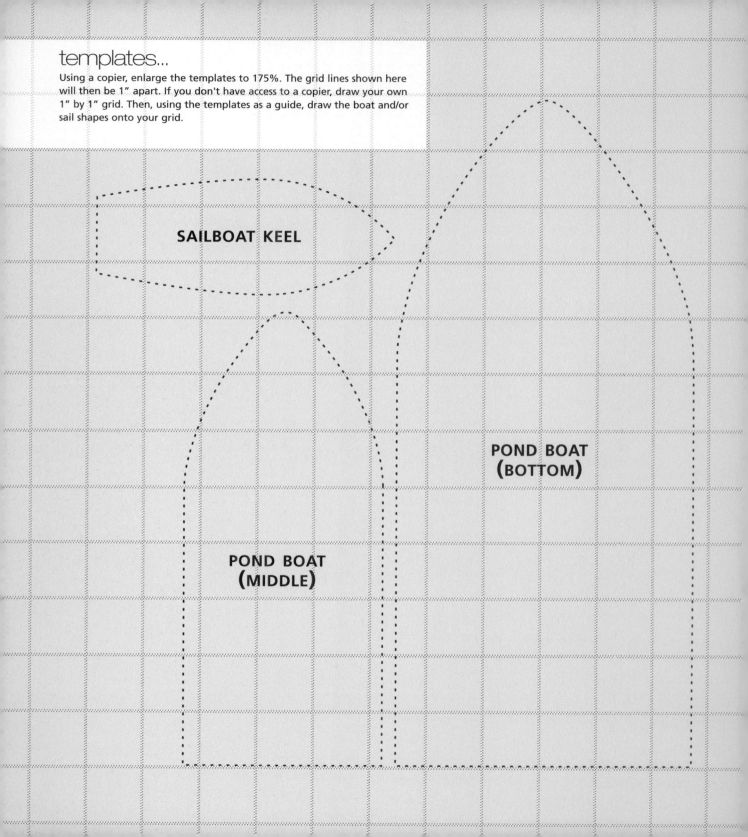

templates...

Using a copier, enlarge the templates to 175%. The grid lines shown here will then be 1" apart. If you don't have access to a copier, draw your own 1" by 1" grid. Then, using the templates as a guide, draw the boat and/or sail shapes onto your grid.

SAILBOAT KEEL

POND BOAT (BOTTOM)

POND BOAT (MIDDLE)

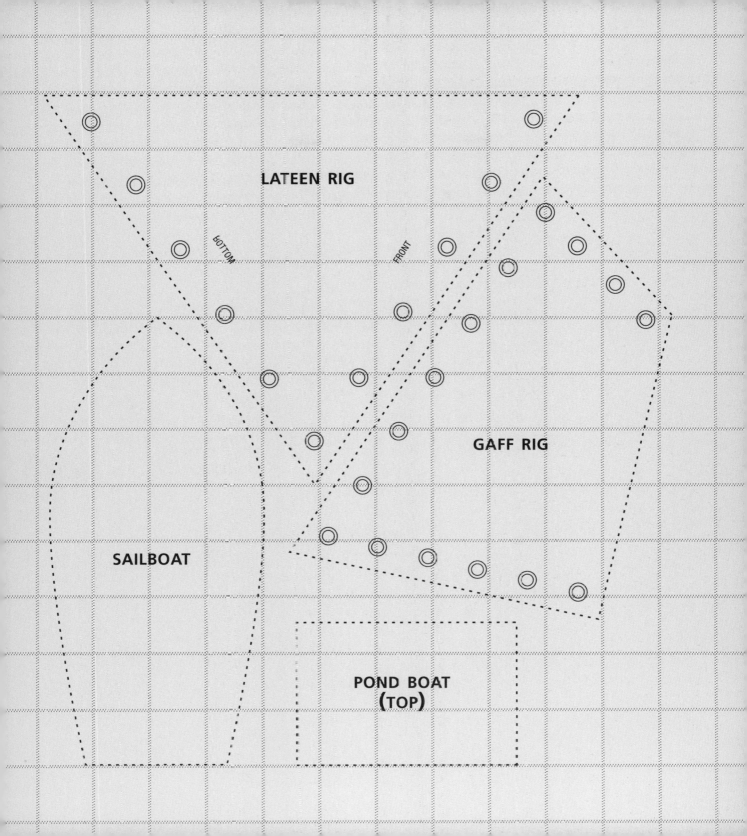

templates...

Using a copier, enlarge the templates for the dolls to 150%. The grid lines shown here will then be 1" apart. If you don't have access to a copier, draw your own 1" by 1" grid. Then, using the templates as a guide, draw the mermaid doll shapes onto your grid. If you want to make the merman and mermaid pillow set, enlarge those templates to whatever size you like.

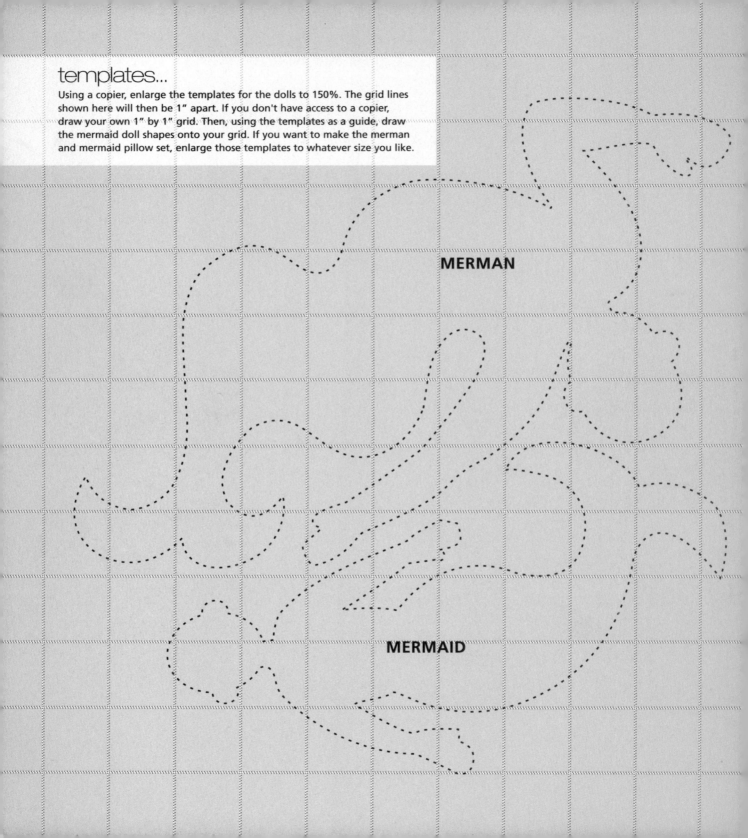

MERMAN

MERMAID